PROTECT

PURITY

Four Keys to Guarding Your Heart

DON SISK

First published in 2013 by Striving Together Publications, a ministry
of Lancaster Baptist Church, Lancaster, CA 93535. Striving Together
Publications is committed to providing tried, trusted, and proven
resources that will further equip local churches to carry out the
Great Commission. Your comments and suggestions are valued.

Striving Together Publications
4020 E. Lancaster Blvd.
Lancaster, CA 93535
800.201.7748
www.strivingtogether.com

Cover design by Andrew Hutchens
Layout by Craig Parker
Edited by Rob Byers
Special thanks to our proofreaders

The author and publication team have put forth every effort to give proper
credit to quotes and thoughts that are not original with the author. It is not
our intent to claim originality with any quote or thought that could not
readily be tied to an original source.

ISBN 978–1-59894–234–7
Printed in the United States of America

Contents

Introduction
A Study in Contrasts

Two men. Two backgrounds. Two sets of opportunities. Two responses. And two vastly separated outcomes.

The first was a young man separated from home, family, culture, language—all of the props of his identity. Furthermore, he had no visible presence of God and no tangible place of worship to remind him to do right. He had a simple, rustic background, but he was thrown into a complex and demeaning system in which he had to learn to thrive to survive.

The other man was more mature and was surrounded by the trappings of power. He even lived near the Ark of the Covenant.

The first man had endured significant hardships and suffering, including betrayal by his own family and living as a slave. The second had gone through a period of persecution but had risen to power and was a king.

The first man had no access to the Word of God. The second had the Law of Moses to instruct his behavior.

Both men were confronted with moral temptation. Knowing the facts about their lives, which do you think gave in to lust?

We would most likely assume that the first man—the one without family, relationships, and accountability, the one without the written Word of God, the one who was personally vulnerable and unprotected—would be the one to yield to temptation. But he did not.

The two men are Joseph and David.

Joseph could have easily convinced himself that the extremity of his circumstances would justify a little impropriety. But Joseph maintained his purity, even though he was thrown into prison as a result.

On the other hand, David should have allowed his many blessings to convince him to resist temptation and to do right. But David sacrificed his purity, and it brought death and suffering to his family.

Reading the Scripture accounts of these two men together helps us understand how we can stay pure, even in a polluted world.

> *And it came to pass after these things, that his master's wife cast her eyes upon Joseph; and she said, Lie with me. But he refused, and said unto his master's wife, Behold, my master wotteth not what is with me in the house, and he hath committed all that he hath to my hand; There is none greater in this house than I; neither hath he kept back any thing from me but thee, because thou art his wife: how then can I do this great wickedness, and sin against God? And it came to pass, as she spake to Joseph day by day, that he hearkened not unto her,*

to lie by her, or to be with her. And it came to pass about this time, that Joseph went into the house to do his business; and there was none of the men of the house there within. And she caught him by his garment, saying, Lie with me: and he left his garment in her hand, and fled, and got him out.
—Genesis 39:7–12

And it came to pass, after the year was expired, at the time when kings go forth to battle, that David sent Joab, and his servants with him, and all Israel; and they destroyed the children of Ammon, and besieged Rabbah. But David tarried still at Jerusalem. And it came to pass in an eveningtide, that David arose from off his bed, and walked upon the roof of the king's house: and from the roof he saw a woman washing herself; and the woman was very beautiful to look upon. And David sent and enquired after the woman. And one said, Is not this Bathsheba, the daughter of Eliam, the wife of Uriah the Hittite? And David sent messengers, and took her; and she came in unto him, and he lay with her; for she was purified from her uncleanness: and she returned unto her house. And the woman

conceived, and sent and told David, and said, I am
with child.—2 SAMUEL 11:1–5

A decision made in a moment of temptation and crisis kept Joseph's purity intact. A decision made in a moment of temptation and crisis destroyed David's purity. The consequences of their decisions shaped the course of the rest of their lives.

The immediate aftermath of Joseph's refusal of temptation was devastating—he was thrown into prison. But in the end, it was simply part of God's plan to bring him before Pharaoh, to elevate him to rule in Egypt. He was then able to save Jacob and his family from the great famine.

The immediate aftermath of David's yielding to temptation appeared to be the perfect cover-up—although it cost the life of one of David's bravest warriors. Yet it was not long before Nathan was sent by God to confront David and force him to face the consequences of his sin. Though David remained king over Israel, his life was changed forever by his few moments of pleasure with Bathsheba. The prophet

Nathan told David, "Now therefore the sword shall never depart from thine house" (2 Samuel 12:10). The toll taken by sin that followed in David's life was devastating to him and to his family: the baby conceived in adultery died shortly after birth. David's daughter Tamar was raped by his son Amnon. Amnon was murdered by his half-brother Absalom. Absalom instigated a public rebellion against David.

The old saying is true: "Sin will take you further than you want to go, keep you longer than you want to stay, and cost you more than you want to pay."

David is probably my favorite character in the whole Bible, but it breaks my heart to read this episode of his life. Joseph's story of similar temptation is a joy because it tells of one person's victory followed by God's miraculous and sovereign blessing.

So what was the difference? Why did young Joseph succeed and older David fail? Why did the "man after God's own heart" commit murder and adultery while the slave boy went to prison rather than give up his purity? To answer these questions, we need to look at the temptation that each of them faced.

Chapter One
Facts about Temptation

D uke Raynard III ruled in the fourteenth century over much of what is now Belgium. Most of the people called him by a nickname—Crassus, the Latin word for *fat*—because he was so overweight.

Raynard's younger brother, Edward, eventually led a successful revolt and took the throne. Although he captured Raynard, Edward refused to kill him. Instead, he devised a most unusual arrangement.

He built a new room inside the castle around his brother. The doors and windows were not locked or barred, and Edward told Raynard that he was free to leave at any time. But, knowing his brother's appetite, Edward had arranged for the doors and windows to be slightly smaller than normal size. As a result, Raynard could not fit through them unless he lost weight.

Each day, Edward sent plates of delicious food to his brother. Every day his brother continued to eat, thus denying himself freedom. Edward told the people of the kingdom, "My brother is not a prisoner. He may leave when he so wills." But ten years passed, and Raynard was still trapped in that room, unwilling to resist the temptation of food. Finally Edward was killed in battle, and the walls were knocked down to allow Raynard out. By then, his health was so poor that he died not long after. He did not resist temptation, and his life was destroyed as a result.

How different Raynard's life would have been if he had learned to curb his appetite. Yes, it would have been difficult, but it also would have been possible. As much as he enjoyed good food, Raynard's life would have been more enjoyable had he faced his struggle head-on and resisted temptation.

No temptation is impossible.

When we talk about how to maintain purity, it is important that we understand what temptation is, where it comes from, and how it works. The first thing we need to understand is that there is no such thing as a temptation that cannot be resisted.

While there *are* very strong temptations, we never sin unless we willingly go along with the temptation. I've heard people say, "The temptation was so strong that I couldn't resist." Biblically, however, that simply isn't true.

The Bible tells us, "There hath no temptation taken you but such as is common to man: but God is faithful, who will not suffer you to be tempted above that ye are able; but will with the temptation also make a way to escape, that ye may be able to bear it" (1 Corinthians 10:13). Our problem is that, instead of looking for the way of escape, we look for excuses to sin.

Joseph—who, by our thinking, would have had every excuse to sin—instead chose to escape. He didn't

even have an easy escape. In fact, his escape led him
to prison.

David, on the other hand, had only to walk away
from the scene of temptation. No one was holding him
hostage; no one was personally attempting to seduce
him. It was his own lust that kept him from escape.

If we do not take the way of escape, that's not the
devil's fault, nor is it God's fault. The fault for every
sin lies in our own hearts. James said, "But every man
is tempted, when he is drawn away of his own lust,
and enticed" (James 1:14).

Temptation strikes a broad range of targets.

Temptation is a problem for every age. Joseph was a
young man probably still in his teens when Potiphar's
wife attempted to seduce him. David was an older
man in his middle age when he saw Bathsheba from
the rooftop. No one is exempt from the allure of sin
because of their youth or their age.

Temptation is not limited by geography. Joseph was hundreds of miles away from his home and family when his moment of testing arose. David was at home in his palace. You can be tempted to sin just as easily in church as you can at work or at home. There aren't any safe places where you can relax and let down your guard. Peter put it this way: "Be sober, be vigilant; because your adversary the devil, as a roaring lion, walketh about, seeking whom he may devour: Whom resist stedfast in the faith, knowing that the same afflictions are accomplished in your brethren that are in the world" (1 Peter 5:8–9).

Temptation seeks vulnerability.

As a crafty hunter, Satan strikes when we are in our most vulnerable moments.

Joseph—although it was certainly not by his own choice—was removed from the authority figures in his life. He had no father, older brothers, or spiritual leader to answer to. There was no one to check up on him to see if he was doing what was right or even to know if he was doing wrong. There was no one to encourage him to avoid temptation and maintain his purity. That was a dangerous place to be spiritually, and Satan targeted it with skill.

David was in a similar position. He had been blessed by God in great ways, but when it was time for kings to go to battle, he stayed behind. He was separated from his friends and his mighty men. Once again, Satan capitalized on David's place of danger.

Too often, we let down our guard during times of prosperity. As we receive God's blessings and become successful, we have a tendency to cut ourselves off from those who would or could help us do right. This makes us more susceptible to temptation.

It goes against our way of thinking, but we are more vulnerable to temptation during prosperity than during adversity. And the worst part about it is that we are generally unaware of our increased vulnerability. This is why Paul warned, "Wherefore let him that thinketh he standeth take heed lest he fall" (1 Corinthians 10:12).

We do not outgrow temptation.

Temptation is not just a "young man's battle." When Paul instructed Timothy, "Flee also youthful lusts" (2 Timothy 2:22), Timothy was not a teenager. Second Timothy was Paul's final epistle which was written from prison in Rome not long before Paul was executed by Nero. By that time, Timothy would have been much older—yet "youthful lusts" were still a danger. We do not outgrow temptation, and we must remain on guard if we want to maintain our purity.

Temptation is not a sin.

One final—but vital—fact to remember regarding temptation: *temptation is not a sin.* The fact that you're tempted does not mean you have already sinned and may as well just give in. Actually, the fact you're tempted means you should quickly rush for the "way of escape" that is promised by God.

Joseph was tempted, but he did not sin. He chose to flee. David sinned, but his sin was not in seeing Bathsheba bathing. David's sin was when he kept looking. As David continued to look at Bathsheba, his lust grew. Eventually he reached the point when, even though he knew she was the wife of one of his best friends, Uriah the Hittite, he didn't care. That would never have happened if David had simply stopped looking.

We can't have complete control over what we see, but we can determine what we look at. Ultimately, it is our willingness to entertain temptation that pulls us into its awful trap.

Alexander Pope skillfully described how familiarity with sin weakens our sensitivity:

> Vice is a monster of so frightful mien
> As to be hated needs but to be seen;
> Yet seen too oft, familiar with her face,
> We first endure, then pity, then embrace.

We've seen a few of the similarities between the temptations that both Joseph and David faced. Why then was the outcome in their lives so different? Why did Joseph stand and David fall when Joseph faced greater obstacles by doing right? Why did Joseph's purity remain protected although it would seem that Joseph was in a much more vulnerable position than David?

The difference is simple: Joseph had fences, and David didn't.

Chapter Two
Building Fences to Protect Purity

When the Union Army under General Sherman was marching through South Carolina, they captured the city of Cheraw. In their haste to flee, the Confederate troops left behind huge stores of gunpowder. Union troops began to carry handfuls of it away to the camp. There they would throw the gunpowder into the cooking fires of unsuspecting fellow soldiers, creating a quick explosion.

What they did not realize was that as they made their trips, they were dropping grains of gunpowder through their fingers…leaving an explosive trail behind. Sergeant Theodore Upson of the 100th Indiana Infantry later recorded the scene. Just after he put his coffee on to boil, he saw "a little flash of powder running along the ground." Someone shouted, "Look out for the magazine!" Upson then wrote that there was a tremendous explosion and dirt and stones flew in every direction.

The cannon balls and artillery shells stored in the weapons magazine exploded with a blast that shook the ground for miles. Several buildings were destroyed, and at least four soldiers were killed and many more wounded. It seemed like harmless fun, but careless choices caused tremendous damage and loss of life. It is the same way when we face temptation.

Joseph's integrity was not instantly forged in the moment Potiphar's wife grabbed him and propositioned him. Joseph already had integrity because of choices he had made in the days, months, and years before that moment. He had built fences that protected him in his most vulnerable moments.

These fences do not require an engineering degree to construct. They simply require an obedience to the Lord and a desire to remain pure before Him.

As we look at the fences in Joseph's life, I challenge you to build similar fences in your heart and life.

Fence #1: Develop convictions before the point of temptation.

If you wait to draw a line for yourself until the moment you are enticed, you are likely to give in to sin. Instead, do as Daniel did when he was carried away into Babylonian captivity. *Before* Daniel was faced with the choice to defile himself, he made a decision: "But Daniel purposed in his heart that he would not defile himself with the portion of the king's meat, nor with the wine which he drank…" (Daniel 1:8).

The place of temptation is no place to determine your convictions and standards. Purpose in your heart ahead of time that you will remain pure. Set standards in place and guard them.

Joseph lived long before the Ten Commandments were given to Moses on Mt. Sinai with the prohibition on adultery. Yet Joseph had learned what was right and what was wrong, and he had determined that he would do right. He told Potiphar's wife, "How then can I do this great wickedness, and sin against God?"

I have watched young people over the years stand and make a promise to God, to their families, and to the church that they will remain pure before the Lord. Does that mean they won't be tempted? No, they will be tempted—perhaps more so because Satan will try to derail that commitment. Yet when the moment of temptation comes, they have something on which to fall back upon. They will remember the moment they promised God they would keep themselves pure for their future spouse. It helps to determine that ahead of time.

If you make a commitment to be pure in our society today, you are going against the grain. People are going to call you old-fashioned. That's not a problem. We don't have to live in the gutter with the rest of the world. One godly Christian man who served in the army during the Korean War told of his experience. On the weekends, many of the soldiers would take a truck into town to visit the prostitutes who were readily available. On Monday, many of those same men rode the bus to the medical tent to get treatment for the diseases they had contracted from their immoral behavior. By skipping the truck, he skipped the bus too!

God's plan is for us to be pure. People often talk to me about how they can know God's will for their lives. I don't know every detail of His plan for you, but I do know this—He intends for you to be pure. Paul wrote, "For this is the will of God, even your sanctification, that ye should abstain from fornication" (1 Thessalonians 4:3).

Incidentally, purity is not just a pre-marriage virtue. Every husband and every wife should be committed to protecting the promise they made to God and to each other when they got married. Hebrews 13:4 says, "Marriage is honourable in all, and the bed undefiled: but whoremongers and adulterers God will judge."

If marriage was man's idea, then man could make the rules. We see a lot of people trying to do that in our day. They don't like the restrictions God has put in place, so they are trying to come up with new plans for marriage and new definitions for the term. But marriage is God's plan. It was His idea from the beginning of creation, and His rule is one man and one woman married faithfully to each other until death do they part. "And said, For this cause shall a man leave father and mother, and shall cleave to his wife: and they twain shall be one flesh? Wherefore they are no more twain, but one flesh. What therefore God hath joined together, let not man put asunder" (Matthew 19:5–6).

Our world may have changed what it regards as acceptable behavior. Today, people seem to think that if there are two consenting adults involved it doesn't matter what they do. We call an adulterous relationship an "affair"—making it sound like something light and fun. But, in fact, it is an enormous betrayal that produces devastating results not just for the people involved, but their spouses, children, and ministries as well. The few moments of illicit pleasure leave a lifetime of regret.

Physical intimacy outside of the bounds of holy matrimony is always great wickedness. It produces devastating results, whether we're talking about two teenagers in the back of a car or someone who is breaking the bonds of a thirty-year marriage.

It is time for God's children to determine that they are going to quit listening to the world, the television, the magazines, and their friends when it comes to choices regarding marriage and purity. God's Word makes the choices clear, but we must chose biblical convictions for ourselves.

Marital purity does not happen by accident. If you are not specifically and intentionally working on guarding your purity, you are in grave danger. I believe it is valuable for spouses to regularly say to each other, "I will never be unfaithful to you." Remember the security of your spouse verbalizing those vows on your wedding day? Verbalize them to one another throughout your lives together.

Though the temptations may be strong, by the grace of God and the power of the Holy Spirit, you can stay pure—whether you are single or married.

Satan is a master at pointing to the green grass on the other side of the fence, and many people fall because they become fixated on forbidden pleasures.

The devil says, "Look at that apple. It is so delicious." Of course, he knows there is a worm right in the middle of it, but as long as he can keep that hidden from your view until you take the first bite, he will be happy.

The longer you look at that apple, the better it looks. But if you have made up your mind before the apple is presented, you will find it much easier to decline the diseased apple.

Joseph was not any different from us. He had the same human nature that we do. He had the hormones of a young man, and the temptation was real. Joseph did not succeed in maintaining his purity because he wasn't tested—I'm sure that there was part of him that was flattered by Potiphar's wife and her interest in him. Yet Joseph did not give in, and it was in large part because of the decisions he had made before that moment of temptation came.

Joseph recognized that in the final analysis keeping his purity was first and foremost about his relationship with God. He said, "How then can I do this great wickedness and sin against God?" Immoral behavior is not just an offense against your current or future spouse and against yourself; worst of all, it is an offense against the high and holy God of Heaven.

Fence #2: Recognize that love involves commitment.

We sometimes think of this temptation Joseph faced as a one-time sudden event when he did what was right in a moment of crisis. The Bible, however, paints a different picture. Potiphar's wife had set her eyes on Joseph because he was young and good looking, and so she set out on a campaign to seduce him. Scripture records that she talked to him "day by day." Joseph did not reject Potiphar's wife once; he had to say "no" again and again.

I've heard of moral failures by men who had worked for God for many years. People often say something like, "He just suddenly ran off with a woman in the church." It doesn't happen like that. It is a process that takes time.

Someone said, "Backsliding is not a blowout. It's a slow leak." Moral failure doesn't happen overnight. Instead, it is something that unfolds over time as temptation is tolerated rather than rejected. The longer we wait to walk away, the easier it becomes for us to give up our commitment.

In almost every case of moral failure where I have known the details of the situation, there was pornography involved before the decision to commit physical fornication or adultery. A man who convinces himself it isn't cheating to look and lust in private has already broken his commitment to God and to his current or future spouse. It isn't a big step from there to go the rest of the way and to turn that secret desire for illicit fulfillment into physical immorality.

The commitment that you make to do right and be pure has to be maintained and guarded day after day. You do not stay pure by making one promise in your youth, or even middle age, that you will do right. You have to keep and protect that commitment day after day after day. It will be tested. Just because you successfully resist temptation today, you should not expect to be free from pressure tomorrow. The devil is patient because he knows that people often do right for a while and then relax because they think that they are safe.

Perhaps you have had the experience of visiting the kind of wild animal park where you drive through the park and watch the animals from your car. When you enter the lion area, they have a sign that says "Do not lower your windows even one inch—that may be too much!" Now, if you are like me, when you see a sign like that you check every window twice to make sure they are completely closed.

It is the same way with Satan. A tiny opening is all that he needs to bring death and destruction into your life. The "innocent" conversations you have been having with someone at work that are starting to last longer and longer are a lowering of your commitment to purity. You haven't yet crossed a line, but you are rolling down the window. The pictures you have saved on your computer that you look at when no one else is awake are across the line, but you may be deceived into thinking that you are still in control when, in fact, you are in deadly peril.

If you have been compromising your commitment to purity, take this book as a last-chance warning. It's time now for thorough repentance and change before it's too late. No matter what the cost, take steps to protect yourself, honor your spouse (present or future), and obey your God.

If it means giving up a job to protect your purity, it is worth it. If you can't control the computer, unplug it. Do whatever it takes. Sin is serious business, and drastic measures are not unwarranted.

Listen to how Jesus described it:

> *Wherefore if thy hand or thy foot offend thee, cut them off, and cast them from thee: it is better for thee to enter into life halt or maimed, rather than having two hands or two feet to be cast into*

everlasting fire. And if thine eye offend thee, pluck it out, and cast it from thee: it is better for thee to enter into life with one eye, rather than having two eyes to be cast into hell fire.—MATTHEW 18:8–9

The world's advice today would run more along the lines of getting a good pair of sunglasses than plucking out an eye. But the world does not take sin seriously, and much of our problem in the church is that we don't either. Your commitment to purity only helps protect you as long as you keep and maintain it.

Fence #3: Refuse to become comfortable with sin.

One of the most noticeable aspects of this passage is that Joseph kept his ability to be shocked at sin. Although Potiphar's wife was on a purposeful campaign to wear Joseph down, he never lost his repugnance for sin.

Sin is an awful thing, and it is a tragedy that we have gotten so used to it. I've heard people say, "Nothing shocks me anymore." I hope that never becomes true of me. I want to keep my heart soft and my conscience clean so that sin always remains awful to me. That helps me do right.

Joseph said immorality was "great wickedness"— and he was right. It is a horrible betrayal and sin against God. Sin is serious business.

Look at how Nehemiah responded when he faced a sin problem in his day:

> *In those days also saw I Jews that had married wives of Ashdod, of Ammon, and of Moab: And their children spake half in the speech of Ashdod, and could not speak in the Jews' language, but according to the language of each people. And I contended with them, and cursed them, and smote certain of them, and plucked off their hair, and made them swear by God, saying, Ye shall not give your daughters unto their sons, nor take their daughters unto your sons, or for yourselves. Did not Solomon king of Israel sin by these things? yet among many nations was there no king like him, who was beloved of his God, and God made him king over all Israel: nevertheless even him*

did outlandish women cause to sin. Shall we then hearken unto you to do all this great evil, to transgress against our God in marrying strange wives?—NEHEMIAH 13:23–27

Now I've heard some pretty hard preaching about sin over the years, and I've watched preachers confront people who were sinning and needed to change their ways. But I can assure you that I've never seen anyone grab a sinner and pull out his hair! I'm not suggesting that as a model for counseling, but I am saying that there is an enormous need for us to be shocked, astonished, and outraged by sin instead of growing used to it.

The sad truth is that you undoubtedly have personally known people who have traded their purity for the temporary pleasure of immorality. I do as well. But I also know many people who haven't. Just because some Christians sin does not mean that everyone is doing wrong or that no one can be trusted. There are many believers who are doing right and honoring God. And even if you were the only one standing firm, it would still be the right thing to do. Do not allow the failure of others or the world's casual attitude toward sin to infect your thinking.

Keep sin "exceeding sinful" (Romans 7:13) in your thoughts, and you will have a powerful protection against doing wrong. The world may make light of sin and treat it as no big deal, but we should treat it like the poisonous and destructive force that it is. God still hates sin and we should as well.

Fence #4: Value your purity above pleasure.

Joseph knew that retreat was better than defeat. When all else fails, run! Joseph had been steadfast in his refusal to submit to the temptation of Potiphar's wife. But the day came when she took advantage of the fact that he was alone with her in the house and grabbed him by his coat. When he saw that, he left his coat in her hand and fled. It cost him a coat, and it was used as evidence to get him thrown into prison, but to Joseph, it was worth it to keep his integrity. He was able to go to prison with a clear conscience. He might have been falsely accused—he couldn't do anything about that—but he knew he had done right.

Paul gave a similar exhortation to Timothy regarding purity: "Flee also youthful lusts" (2 Timothy 2:22). Of all the words Paul could have used to instruct Timothy away from lusts, notice what he did not use—*walk, stroll, turn from, step, ramble.* He firmly said "Flee!"

The Greek word that is used here means "to run to safety." It is the word you would use to describe the soldiers of a defeated army trying to escape from the battlefield. This is not a casual word but an urgent one. When lust and temptation show up, get out fast and do whatever it takes to flee the danger.

Guard your fences.

The Great Wall of China is the largest man-made object on earth. In fact, it is so big that it is visible from outer space! Yet the wall, much of which was built in the 1400s during the Ming Dynasty to protect against invasions, did not prove to be a solution. Guards were often bribed to open the gates, rendering the wall ineffective. During one rebellion, a general threw open the gates in hopes that the invading Manchu forces would scatter the rebellion. Instead, they conquered the city of Beijing. Your fences will do you no good unless you both build *and* guard them.

In contrast to Joseph and his successful stand against temptation, let's look back at David. I do believe that David had made a commitment to do right. We do not know for certain who wrote Psalm 119, but the words of Psalm 119:11 are ones I believe David would have echoed from his heart: "Thy word have I hid in mine heart, that I might not sin against thee." David's heart was in the right place when he started out.

There are many examples from earlier in his life when he could have violated God's law and everyone would have thought that he was fully justified, but he refused. When Saul slept in the cave where David was hiding, David's men wanted him to kill the king who was unjustly seeking his life, but David refused. He had made a commitment to do right, but he did not continue to maintain it.

Before David committed adultery, he began abandoning his other commitments. The Bible tells us, that though it was "the time when kings went forth to battle," David was sitting at home in the palace in Jerusalem. The Bible does not tell us why David remained behind. Considering his tender heart toward God, I do not believe it was his intention to violate God's law and ruin his future. In fact, I suspect that if you had told David what was coming, he would have been at the head of the troops on their way out of town.

But when we abandon one commitment, it is easier for us to abandon the next one. The famed football coach Bear Bryant told his players: "The first time you quit it's hard. But every time after that it gets easier and easier." Keep all of the commitments you have made to God. Whether it is tithing, daily Bible reading, church attendance, faithfulness in your witness, or something else, each commitment you keep helps to protect your commitment to purity.

One of the biggest problems David had was that he was not shocked by the idea of sin. When he saw Bathsheba bathing on the roof of her house as he looked out from the palace, he did not know who she was. Make no mistake, no matter who she was, David should not have been lusting after her. Yet she was not a random stranger but the wife of Uriah. That should have meant something to David.

During the time when David was running from King Saul, he was joined by a large group of men who journeyed and fought with him. Among that group of several hundred, there were a few dozen who distinguished themselves by their courage and cunning in battle. These were known as "David's mighty men," and among their number, named in 1 Chronicles 11, is Uriah the Hittite.

He was a member of David's inner circle—those most trusted and relied on. If his commitment to God and to his responsibilities were not enough to help David overcome temptation, this should have shocked him back to his senses. The idea that he was even thinking of taking the wife of one of his best and bravest soldiers should have stopped David in his tracks, but it didn't. Instead, he sent his servants to have Bathsheba brought to the palace, and David committed a horrible sin.

How much different and better David's life would have been if he had done as Joseph did and fled from the temptation he faced! Instead he treated sin casually.

Then once the consequences of his first sin became apparent and Bathsheba told him she was pregnant, David went further. After a futile attempt to get Uriah to go home to his wife in hopes that he could be presented as the father of the child. But Uriah was honorable and kept his commitment, unlike his king, so David arranged for Uriah to be killed in battle so that he could take Bathsheba for himself.

It appeared to David that he had successfully managed to cover his tracks. He did not, however, account for one thing—God. The Bible says, "But the thing that David had done displeased the LORD" (2 Samuel 11:27). God refused to allow David to cover his sin and get away with it...and the same is not going to be different for you. If you make the horrible decision to sacrifice your purity and honor for the sake of temporary pleasure, God is going to bring the consequences down upon your head. It is far better to maintain your integrity and to do right.

Perhaps the past already holds soiled memories for you. Perhaps, like David, you have let down your fences.

We have a loving God who gives us second chances. He offers His forgiveness if we will own up to our responsibility and confess our sin to Him.

> *If we say that we have no sin, we deceive ourselves, and the truth is not in us. If we confess our sins, he is faithful and just to forgive us our sins, and to cleanse us from all unrighteousness.*—1 JOHN 1:8–9

The writer of Proverbs pointed out that to cover our sin is disastrous; to confess and forsake it is cleansing: "He that covereth his sins shall not prosper: but whoso confesseth and forsaketh them shall have mercy" (Proverbs 28:13).

This is always true with God, and it is often true with others as well. If you hide moral sin from your spouse, it is like ignoring broken fences in a relationship. If with sincere repentance you confess your sin and take thorough measures to forsake it, you are far more likely to restore your relationship.

Yes, there will always be scars. David's life is a perfect example of this. He received forgiveness, but for the rest of his life, he suffered severe consequences for his sin. Yet, His relationship with God was restored, and he was able to once again know the joy of his salvation.

Regardless of the past, I challenge you today to begin a life of purity.

The triumph of Joseph and the tragedy of David remind us of the importance of establishing fences to protect us from temptation. They also show us the importance of guarding and protecting those fences so that we can resist and overcome temptation and maintain our purity.

Chapter Three
Fulfilling God-Given Appetites God's Way

P art of the reason that purity is such a problem for so many is that we have, in large measure, adopted the attitude of the world toward physical intimacy. When God created man, He gave us certain appetites and desires. The desires themselves are not wrong, nor are the means that God has given us by which those appetites can be fulfilled. The problem comes when we try to fulfill those appetites apart from the means which God has ordained for their fulfillment.

For example, God made man to desire food. God told Adam and Eve that they could eat the fruit that grew on any of the trees in the Garden of Eden, except for the Tree of the Knowledge of Good and Evil. God not only gave them the appetite for food, but He provided a legitimate means by which that need could be met. As long as Adam and Eve didn't eat the fruit of the one forbidden tree, there was no problem. There was no sin in the desire to eat or in eating anything that God had allowed them to.

The devil's plan then, just as it is now, was to get Adam and Eve to meet a legitimate need in some other way other that was not God's way.

Likewise, this was the heart of Satan's temptation of Christ. He tried to get Jesus to use His power to feed Himself, to presume on God's protection to make Himself famous, and to acquire power over the world through false worship. Jesus having food, being protected, and receiving power were all good things—but they had to be done in God's way in order to be right.

*Then was Jesus led up of the Spirit into the wilderness to be tempted of the devil. And when he had fasted forty days and forty nights, he was afterward an hungred. And when the tempter came to him, he said, If thou be the Son of God, command that these stones be made bread. But he answered and said, It is written, Man shall not live by bread alone, but by every word that proceedeth out of the mouth of God. Then the devil taketh him up into the holy city, and setteth him on a pinnacle of the temple, And saith unto him, If thou be the Son of God, cast thyself down: for it is written, He shall give his angels charge concerning thee: and in their hands they shall bear thee up, lest at any time thou dash thy foot against a stone. Jesus said unto him, It is written again, Thou shalt not tempt the Lord thy God. Again, the devil taketh him up into an exceeding high mountain, and sheweth him all the kingdoms of the world, and the glory of them; And saith unto him, All these things will I give thee, if thou wilt fall down and worship me. Then saith Jesus unto him, Get thee hence, Satan: for it is written, Thou shalt worship the Lord thy God, and him only shalt thou serve.—*Matthew 4:1–10

God created the desire for intimacy just as He did the desire for food. And just as He did with food, He also gave us a legitimate means of meeting that desire. God's plan for our sexual satisfaction is for a husband and a wife to join together for life and meet one another's needs. There is no sin in the desire for intimacy, provided that we are willing to meet that desire only in the way God has ordained.

When God looked over His creation, He pronounced everything that He had made as being "good." Yet when God considered the situation, He found one thing that was not satisfactory—and He did something about it. "And the LORD God said, It is not good that the man should be alone; I will make him an help meet for him…And the LORD God caused a deep sleep to fall upon Adam, and he slept: and he took one of his ribs, and closed up the flesh instead thereof; And the rib, which the LORD God had taken from man, made he a woman, and brought her unto the man" (Genesis 2:18, 21–22).

Intimacy is not a human invention—it is God's idea. And we should not allow the fact that the world has twisted and perverted God's plan to keep us from following it. God designed marriage for a number of reasons, but one of them is for this sexual appetite that He has given to us to be met. When this appetite is fulfilled in the way God intended, it is a beautiful thing.

> *Drink waters out of thine own cistern, and running waters out of thine own well. Let thy fountains be dispersed abroad, and rivers of waters in the streets. Let them be only thine own, and not strangers' with thee. Let thy fountain be blessed: and rejoice with the wife of thy youth. Let her be as the loving hind and pleasant roe; let her breasts satisfy thee at all times; and be thou ravished always with her love. And why wilt thou, my son, be ravished with a strange woman, and embrace the bosom of a stranger? For the ways of man are before the eyes of the LORD, and he pondereth all his goings. His own iniquities shall take the wicked himself, and he shall be holden with the cords of his sins. He shall die without instruction; and in the greatness of his folly he shall go astray.*—PROVERBS 5:15–23

In these words from Proverbs, we see a description of God's idea. We see a powerful declaration that sexual fulfillment is only to be found within the bounds of marriage, as well as a strong warning of what happens when we go outside those boundaries. Intimacy within marriage is honorable and right (Hebrews 13:4). In fact, each person who is married has a responsibility to do their best to meet the needs of their spouse.

I am not in any way saying it is the wife's fault if the husband is immoral or vice versa—each of us is responsible to do right no matter what. If your desires and needs are not being met in your marriage, that does not excuse you in any way to be immoral in order to try to get those needs met. Joseph had been horribly mistreated by his brothers and sold as a slave, but that did not justify committing adultery with Potiphar's wife.

> *Now concerning the things whereof ye wrote unto me: It is good for a man not to touch a woman. Nevertheless, to avoid fornication, let every man*

have his own wife, and let every woman have her own husband. Let the husband render unto the wife due benevolence: and likewise also the wife unto the husband. The wife hath not power of her own body, but the husband: and likewise also the husband hath not power of his own body, but the wife. Defraud ye not one the other, except it be with consent for a time, that ye may give yourselves to fasting and prayer; and come together again, that Satan tempt you not for your incontinency.
—1 CORINTHIANS 7:1–5

Marital intimacy should never be viewed as a reward or a weapon. A husband has a responsibility to meet his wife's physical needs, and a wife has the same responsibility toward her husband. There is a very strong statement here—our bodies do not belong to us. We are not to selfishly seek our own pleasure or desire, but instead to seek the pleasure of our spouse. Every married couple needs to devote the time and effort needed to keep their romantic lives warm and happy. Paul says that according to God's design, physical satisfaction within marriage offers us protection from temptation.

Being single, however, does not mean you cannot resist temptation. Joseph and Daniel are two young men whose lives prove that faithfulness to God in the area of moral purity—even without a wife—is possible.

If you are willing to trust God and His plan, you will be both blessed and protected from temptation. This is true in every part of life, but the lesson holds a special force for us in the matter of purity because this is such a powerful way that the enemy attacks.

Conclusion
Keep on Doing Right

L et me share this final warning with you on the matter of purity: you never get too old to be dumb. Someone was asked how old a person had to be before he could stop guarding his thoughts, and he replied, "Ask someone older than me. I'm only eighty."

God has called you to remain pure throughout your life, and with His help and His grace, you can finish your race and win the victory. Yes, many have fallen to immorality. But even more have succeeded in maintaining their honor and their integrity. Your family, your life, and your service to the Lord do not have to be ruined by the lure of temptation.

In *The Odyssey*, Homer told the story of Odysseus and his return home from the battle of Troy. One of the obstacles he had to face was the Sirens. According to Greek mythology, these beautiful singers lured sailors to their death on the rocks with their song. Being warned in advance of the danger, Odysseus plugged the ears of all of his sailors with wax so that they would not be able to hear the tempting song.

But since he wanted to hear the music for himself, Odysseus lashed himself to the mast so that he would not be able to cast himself into the sea and drown when he heard the song. Though Odysseus commanded the crew to release him, signaling wildly to them to set him free, they only bound him more tightly to the mast and continued their journey. Thus Odysseus was able to survive hearing the Sirens' song.

Today, many people foolishly place themselves in a dangerous position. They may think that they are mature enough to handle the temptation without giving in to it. They may think that they will be the exception to the law of sowing and reaping so that they will be able to sin without suffering the consequences. They may think that their service for God exempts them from following all of His rules. All those who think in these ways are tragically wrong, and if they act on the temptations they face, tragedy will result.

Paul recognized that the danger of temptation did not diminish with age and that he faced the risk of undermining everything to which he had devoted his life. He wrote, "But I keep under my body, and bring it into subjection: lest that by any means, when I have preached to others, I myself should be a castaway" (1 Corinthians 9:27). God's plan is for you to do right today, tomorrow, and for the rest of your life. Solomon said that "there is no discharge in that war" (Ecclesiastes 8:8).

The battle against temptation is not one which is ever won completely in this life. A victory today does not guarantee a victory tomorrow. The temptation of Jesus Christ illustrates this truth for us. After Satan had tried three times to get Jesus to meet His legitimate needs in illegitimate ways, did Satan give up? No. The Bible says, "And when the devil had ended all the temptation, he departed from him *for a season*" (Luke 4:13). Any victory you win over temptation is by definition a temporary victory. Don't let down your guard. Don't relax your vigilance. Don't become self-confident. Don't think that you are immune. Paul warned, "Wherefore let him that thinketh he standeth take heed lest he fall" (1 Corinthians 10:12).

Whether you are single or married, the temptation to be impure is the same. No one is exempt or less susceptible than others.

There are lives and souls in the balance, and our purity matters. But this is a battle we can win! God has given us a "way to escape" in every temptation—and if we take that way out, we can and will remain pure.

Helpful Scriptures on Purity

I suggest that you use the Scriptures below in two ways: proactively and defensively.

Proactively, begin committing these verses to memory and meditating on them as you go about your work. Write them on index cards, and carry them with you as you work on them. Perhaps you could memorize them with your dad, your son, or another man with whom you maintain accountability. (You can keep track of which verses you have memorized by writing in the date in the column on the left. If you are working with a partner, you can ask them to initial after you have quoted the verse to him.)

Defensively, review them during moments of temptation. If you already have them memorized, they are much more available for review. But even if you don't have them all memorized, keep them handy—either in this volume or on a list or cards that you carry with you.

God's Word is powerful, and it is the best weapon for defeating lust and defending purity!

❑ _____ JOB 31:1
1 *I made a covenant with mine eyes; why then should I think upon a maid?*

❑ _____ PROVERBS 14:7–9
7 *Go from the presence of a foolish man, when thou perceivest not in him the lips of knowledge.*
8 *The wisdom of the prudent is to understand his way: but the folly of fools is deceit.*
9 *Fools make a mock at sin: but among the righteous there is favour.*

❑ _____ PROVERBS 27:12
12 *A prudent man foreseeth the evil, and hideth himself; but the simple pass on, and are punished.*

❏ ____ PROVERBS 31:30

30 Favour is deceitful, and beauty is vain: but a woman that feareth the Lord, she shall be praised.

❏ ____ ECCLESIASTES 11:9

9 Rejoice, O young man, in thy youth; and let thy heart cheer thee in the days of thy youth, and walk in the ways of thine heart, and in the sight of thine eyes: but know thou, that for all these things God will bring thee into judgment.

❏ ____ ROMANS 6:12–13

12 Let not sin therefore reign in your mortal body, that ye should obey it in the lusts thereof. 13 Neither yield ye your members as instruments of unrighteousness unto sin: but yield yourselves unto God, as those that are alive from the dead, and your members as instruments of righteousness unto God.

❏ ____ ROMANS 13:14

14 But put ye on the Lord Jesus Christ, and make not provision for the flesh, to fulfil the lusts thereof.

❏ ____ GALATIANS 5:24–25

24 And they that are Christ's have crucified the flesh with the affections and lusts. 25 If we live in the Spirit, let us also walk in the Spirit.

❑ ____ JAMES 1:14–15
14 But every man is tempted, when he is drawn away of his own lust, and enticed.
15 Then when lust hath conceived, it bringeth forth sin: and sin, when it is finished, bringeth forth death.

❑ ____ 2 TIMOTHY 2:22
22 Flee also youthful lusts: but follow righteousness, faith, charity, peace, with them that call on the Lord out of a pure heart.

❑ ____ TITUS 2:11–13
11 For the grace of God that bringeth salvation hath appeared to all men,
12 Teaching us that, denying ungodliness and worldly lusts, we should live soberly, righteously, and godly, in this present world;
13 Looking for that blessed hope, and the glorious appearing of the great God and our Saviour Jesus Christ;

❑ ____ HEBREWS 4:13
13 Neither is there any creature that is not manifest in his sight: but all things are naked and opened unto the eyes of him with whom we have to do.

❑ _____ 1 PETER 1:13–15

13 Wherefore gird up the loins of your mind, be sober, and hope to the end for the grace that is to be brought unto you at the revelation of Jesus Christ;

14 As obedient children, not fashioning yourselves according to the former lusts in your ignorance:

15 But as he which hath called you is holy, so be ye holy in all manner of conversation;

❑ _____ 1 PETER 2:11

11 Dearly beloved, I beseech you as strangers and pilgrims, abstain from fleshly lusts, which war against the soul;

❑ _____ 1 PETER 4:1–2

1 Forasmuch then as Christ hath suffered for us in the flesh, arm yourselves likewise with the same mind: for he that hath suffered in the flesh hath ceased from sin;

2 That he no longer should live the rest of his time in the flesh to the lusts of men, but to the will of God.

❑ _____ 1 JOHN 2:16

16 For all that is in the world, the lust of the flesh, and the lust of the eyes, and the pride of life, is not of the Father, but is of the world.

❏ _____   1 JOHN 3:2–3

2 Beloved, now are we the sons of God, and it doth not yet appear what we shall be: but we know that, when he shall appear, we shall be like him; for we shall see him as he is.

3 And every man that hath this hope in him purifieth himself, even as he is pure.

❏ _____   PROVERBS 5:3–23

3 For the lips of a strange woman drop as an honeycomb, and her mouth is smoother than oil:

4 But her end is bitter as wormwood, sharp as a two-edged sword.

5 Her feet go down to death; her steps take hold on hell.

6 Lest thou shouldest ponder the path of life, her ways are moveable, that thou canst not know them.

7 Hear me now therefore, O ye children, and depart not from the words of my mouth.

8 Remove thy way far from her, and come not nigh the door of her house:

9 Lest thou give thine honour unto others, and thy years unto the cruel:

10 Lest strangers be filled with thy wealth; and thy labours be in the house of a stranger;

11 And thou mourn at the last, when thy flesh and thy body are consumed,

12 And say, How have I hated instruction, and my heart despised reproof;

13 And have not obeyed the voice of my teachers, nor inclined mine ear to them that instructed me!

14 I was almost in all evil in the midst of the congregation and assembly.

15 Drink waters out of thine own cistern, and running waters out of thine own well.

16 Let thy fountains be dispersed abroad, and rivers of waters in the streets.

17 Let them be only thine own, and not strangers' with thee.

18 Let thy fountain be blessed: and rejoice with the wife of thy youth.

19 Let her be as the loving hind and pleasant roe; let her breasts satisfy thee at all times; and be thou ravished always with her love.

20 And why wilt thou, my son, be ravished with a strange woman, and embrace the bosom of a stranger?

21 For the ways of man are before the eyes of the Lord, and he pondereth all his goings.

22 His own iniquities shall take the wicked himself, and he shall be holden with the cords of his sins.

23 He shall die without instruction; and in the greatness of his folly he shall go astray.

❑ _____   PROVERBS 6:23–35

23 For the commandment is a lamp; and the law is light; and reproofs of instruction are the way of life:

24 To keep thee from the evil woman, from the flattery of the tongue of a strange woman.

25 Lust not after her beauty in thine heart; neither let her take thee with her eyelids.

26 For by means of a whorish woman a man is brought to a piece of bread: and the adultress will hunt for the precious life.

27 Can a man take fire in his bosom, and his clothes not be burned?

28 Can one go upon hot coals, and his feet not be burned?

29 So he that goeth in to his neighbour's wife; whosoever toucheth her shall not be innocent.

30 Men do not despise a thief, if he steal to satisfy his soul when he is hungry;

31 But if he be found, he shall restore sevenfold; he shall give all the substance of his house.

32 But whoso committeth adultery with a woman lacketh understanding: he that doeth it destroyeth his own soul.

33 A wound and dishonour shall he get; and his reproach shall not be wiped away.

*34 For jealousy is the rage of a man: therefore
he will not spare in the day of vengeance.*
*35 He will not regard any ransom; neither will
he rest content, though thou givest many gifts.*

❑ ____ PROVERBS 7:5–25
*5 That they may keep thee from the strange
woman, from the stranger which flattereth with
her words.*
*6 For at the window of my house I looked
through my casement,*
*7 And beheld among the simple ones, I
discerned among the youths, a young man void
of understanding,*
*8 Passing through the street near her corner;
and he went the way to her house,*
*9 In the twilight, in the evening, in the black
and dark night:*
*10 And, behold, there met him a woman with
the attire of an harlot, and subtil of heart.*
*11 (She is loud and stubborn; her feet abide not
in her house:*
*12 Now is she without, now in the streets, and
lieth in wait at every corner.)*
*13 So she caught him, and kissed him, and with
an impudent face said unto him,*

14 I have peace offerings with me; this day have
I payed my vows.
15 Therefore came I forth to meet thee,
diligently to seek thy face, and I have found thee.
16 I have decked my bed with coverings of
tapestry, with carved works, with fine linen
of Egypt.
17 I have perfumed my bed with myrrh, aloes,
and cinnamon.
18 Come, let us take our fill of love until the
morning: let us solace ourselves with loves.
19 For the goodman is not at home, he is gone a
long journey:
20 He hath taken a bag of money with him,
and will come home at the day appointed.
21 With her much fair speech she caused him
to yield, with the flattering of her lips she
forced him.
22 He goeth after her straightway, as an
ox goeth to the slaughter, or as a fool to the
correction of the stocks;
23 Till a dart strike through his liver; as a bird
hasteth to the snare, and knoweth not that it is
for his life.
24 Hearken unto me now therefore, O ye
children, and attend to the words of my mouth.
25 Let not thine heart decline to her ways, go
not astray in her paths.

❏ _____ PROVERBS 11:2–6

2 When pride cometh, then cometh shame: but with the lowly is wisdom.

3 The integrity of the upright shall guide them: but the perverseness of transgressors shall destroy them.

4 Riches profit not in the day of wrath: but righteousness delivereth from death.

5 The righteousness of the perfect shall direct his way: but the wicked shall fall by his own wickedness.

6 The righteousness of the upright shall deliver them: but transgressors shall be taken in their own naughtiness.

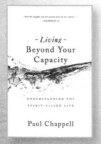

Visit us online

strivingtogether.com

wcbc.edu